NATIONAL MARITIME MUSEUM

SOUVENIR GUIDE

Contents

Different Aspects of Submarines,
from the 'Submarine' series of lithographs by
Eric Ravilious, *c.*1940. PAD8088

Eric Ravilious

Introduction

WELCOME TO THE NATIONAL MARITIME MUSEUM, the world's largest and most-visited museum of seafaring. The Museum's mission is to illustrate for everyone the importance of the sea, ships, time and the stars, and their relationship with people: it has 2.5 million items in its collections including the world's largest specialist maritime library and archive, which are open to researchers of all sorts.

This guide introduces you to the Museum's themes as displayed in its main galleries. The Royal Observatory and Queen's House are our other famous buildings at Greenwich but have separate guidebooks. The Observatory galleries cover astronomy and the measurement of time, which are both closely related to navigation in historical terms. The equally historic Queen's House is the principal showcase for the Museum's art collection.

In January 2012 the Museum, Royal Observatory, Queen's House and the *Cutty Sark* were granted the title of Royal Museums Greenwich, marking HM The Queen's Diamond Jubilee. All aspects of our activities at Greenwich are covered on our website, rmg.co.uk. There you can find information on visiting us, and on our education programmes and research activities – with a steadily increasing proportion of our vast collection also accessible through the Collections Online pages. Other contact details appear inside the back cover here. Enjoy your visit – and come again!

English ships and the Spanish Armada, 1588, contemporary English oil painting on panel. BHC0262

Maritime Greenwich: A World Heritage Site

T HE ELEGANT 'PARK AND PALACE' LANDSCAPE of Greenwich, including the historic town centre around St Alfege's church, became a UNESCO World Heritage Site in December 1997.

To gain this status, a place has to have unique qualities and embody 'outstanding universal values'. Those of Greenwich include its early history as the site of an important royal palace and park (London's oldest); the building of the Observatory in the Park by Charles II in 1675–76 specifically to improve navigation; and construction shortly afterwards of the Royal Hospital for Seamen (now the Old Royal Naval College) where the palace formerly stood.

The Queen's House – the keystone of classical architecture in Britain – is the only significant remnant of the palace. In the early 1800s it became the centre of the school founded by the Royal Hospital in 1712–15. Until the early twentieth century all boys from the school went to sea, latterly in the Royal Navy or Royal Marines, while from 1872 to 1998 the College was the Navy's centre for advanced officer training.

The view north from Greenwich Park, with the Queen's House and linking Museum buildings, the domes of the Old Royal Naval College by the Thames behind, and the London Docklands towers in the distance.

Greenwich therefore has both a royal and a maritime history, especially in relation to its role in British nautical science, charitable welfare and education. This is why, when the Royal Hospital School moved to Suffolk in 1933, its buildings were converted to become the National Maritime Museum (founded in 1934 and opened in 1937). The Observatory was incorporated with the Museum in 1953, following the transfer of its scientific functions elsewhere. The arrival of the *Cutty Sark* for preservation at Greenwich in 1954 rectified one missing element – a truly historic ship. 'Maritime Greenwich' was first used as the title of a guidebook published a little later, and it is a name that World Heritage Site status has rightly confirmed.

The Museum Collections

The Museum, like many others, is above all a 'collection of collections' with thousands of additional items which have arrived individually or in small groups. Much of the overall collection has been generously given, much of it purchased, and some of it is held on loan for various reasons. Apart from loans – and even those when from other public bodies – it is all national property: the Museum only cares for it and holds it in trust for public benefit.

Of our 2.5 million items, the vast majority are documents on paper up to the size of large charts and ship plans, including public records and over a million photographs. 'Objects' number in thousands: for example, there are around 3,300 models, 4,000 oil paintings, over 5,000 navigational and scientific instruments, and more that 25,000 other various items. Most of the 120 boats are now at the National Maritime Museum Cornwall, at Falmouth.

Important historic collections, going back to the eighteenth century, include those from the former Naval Gallery of Greenwich Hospital – paintings, sculpture, and Nelson and Franklin relics – and the former Royal Naval Museum at the Old Royal Naval College (which the Hospital became in 1872): the latter includes the Admiralty collection of ship models.

The greatest and most varied private collection is that amassed for the Museum by its founding benefactor, Sir James Caird: this in itself contains others, such as the huge Macpherson Collection of maritime prints and drawings, the Mercury Collection of ship models, and the Gabb and Barberini Collections of scientific instruments. More recent purchases, with the help of the Heritage Memorial and Heritage Lottery Funds, have included major

WILLIAM IV
BORN 1765
DIED 1837

manuscript and slavery-themed or -linked collections. The Museum's art acquisitions have also been regularly supported since its foundation by the Art Fund and the Macpherson Endowment Fund of the Society for Nautical Research, with many other generous contributors in these and other areas.

The Museum: A Brief History, 1937–2012

The Museum's opening by King George VI on 27 April 1937 was the result of ten years' preparatory work. This began in 1928 when James Caird (1864–1954), a Scottish shipowner and member of the Society for Nautical Research (SNR), bought the Macpherson Collection of maritime prints, drawings and paintings on the understanding it would become the core of a new 'national naval and nautical museum': the title National Maritime Museum was suggested by the writer Rudyard Kipling. Caird was advised by Professor Geoffrey Callender of the Royal Naval College: also prominent in the SNR, he became the Museum's first Director from its foundation by Act of Parliament in 1934 until his death in 1946. Caird also paid for converting the buildings (previously those of the Royal Hospital School), while the historic Queen's House was restored as the heart of the Museum by the Government Office of Works. The Second World War (1939–45) saw the main treasures moved out of London for safekeeping, and post-war advances were slow owing to general austerity. The Admiralty 'Secret Books' department occupied the East Wing during the war and it only came into full Museum use in 1951, with the Royal Observatory incorporated from 1953. By the early 1970s, a comparatively well-resourced period, the Museum was recognized as a world leader in its field. By contrast the 1980s saw radical role reassessments brought on by computerization, renewed financial stringency, and the need for major building works to repair and upgrade the existing structure. The oldest part of the Observatory was restored in the early 1990s and the rest fully redeveloped in 2006–07. Neptune Court, the modern core of the main galleries, was completed in 1999 and complemented in 2011 by the opening of the Sammy Ofer Wing. Including a new library, archive and a modern special exhibitions gallery, this completed at last the full possible utilization of the Museum site, nearly 75 years after its public opening.

The Sammy Ofer Wing, facing Greenwich Park, with the water-steps flanking the café terrace and main entrance. It opened to the public on 14 July 2011.

The Parting Cheer

O VERSEAS MIGRATION from the British Isles began in earnest in the seventeenth century, as settlers voyaged to the recently established English colonies in the New World. The reasons for this emigration were complex: notable 'push factors' were poverty, religious or political persecution, and personal desires; 'pull factors' included the lure of a new life, personal liberty and the chance to prosper.

The scale of emigration grew enormously in the ninteenth century. Between 1815 and 1914, 22.6 million people left Britain. Domestic events like the Irish famine of the 1840s and the Highland Clearances in Scotland spurred great waves of departure, which had a major impact on local populations. Emigration was regarded by many as an essential safety valve that relieved pressure on resources at home. For others, it was a convenient means to rid the country of supposedly idle and politically dangerous classes of people.

The government and other organizations frequently offered help with emigration. They favoured passages to the British settler colonies of Australia, Canada, New Zealand and South Africa. It was the United States of America, however, that attracted the vast majority of British settlers. Events overseas could also lead to sudden peaks in emigration. The various gold rushes of the nineteenth century – California, the Klondike, Victoria, South Africa – famously saw many people, mainly men, depart in search of a quick fortune: only a few were to find it.

O'Neil's *The Parting Cheer* depicts a scene that was all too common in the ports of Victorian Britain, with eager emigrants waving goodbye to those left behind on the quayside. It shows the excitement and sadness of departure that was felt by millions.

The Parting Cheer, by Henry Nelson O'Neil, 1861. Acquired with the assistance of the Heritage Lottery Fund, the Art Fund, and the Friends of the National Maritime Museum. ZBA4022

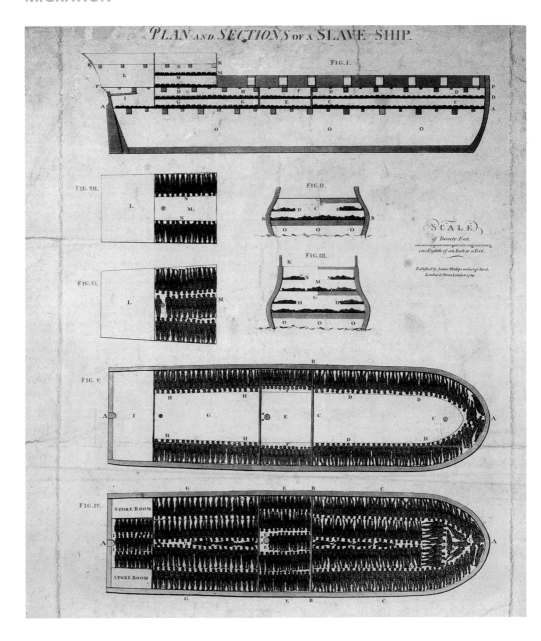

Atlantic Crossings

ABOVE: **Carved ivory tusk**, 19th century. This tusk illustrates scenes on the Loango coast of West Africa. Among other things, it depicts the enslavement of Africans, who are being marched to the coast. ZBA2430

OPPOSITE: *Plan and Sections of a Slave Ship*, published by James Phillips, London, 1789. Phillips was the Quaker publisher for the Society for Effecting the Abolition of the Slave Trade, here reissuing an image first printed in Plymouth in 1788. ZBA2745

WHILE MANY PEOPLE from the British Isles sought fresh opportunities across the Atlantic, British ships also forcibly transported millions of African people to become slave labour on the plantations of the Americas. The lucrative commodities they produced – notably sugar, tobacco and cotton – fed an insatiable demand in Europe and generated huge fortunes. In Britain these provided a significant part of the capital that underpinned the early Industrial Revolution.

This transatlantic slave trade involved most European countries, with around 12 million people torn from their homes and families in Africa. Before 1807, British ships took 3.4 million captive people across the Atlantic. Conditions on board slave ships were appalling. Overcrowding, dehydration and disease produced high mortality: about one in seven Africans died on the Atlantic crossing, and their bodies were simply thrown overboard without any burial rites. Some enslaved people refused food and water, prompting brutal punishment and forced-feeding. Others resisted by organizing violent rebellions.

The dreadful conditions on these ships were later employed in campaigns against the slave trade in Britain. The infamous image of the *Brooks* (opposite) shows this Liverpool slaver carrying 454 captive African people. The depersonalized, geometrically arranged and tightly packed pattern of figures reinforces the grim reality it depicts. The accompanying text explains that the *Brooks* had previously carried over 600 people. Text and illustration together evoke the sheer horror of the so-called 'middle passage'. Ultimately, this image and other evidence of such horrific ship-board conditions presented a powerful case for the complete abolition of the slave trade.

Migration to North America

IN THE CENTURY between the end of the Napoleonic War and the First World War (1815–1914), tens of millions of people left Britain and Europe for North America. It was the biggest mass-migration in history, originally in passenger sailing ships and later in steam vessels. Ships were then the only link between the

Burning of the *Ocean Monarch*, 24 August 1848, watercolour, probably painted by the Prince de Joinville. Just after this emigrant ship left Liverpool for Boston with about 360 migrants on board it caught fire off the Welsh coast and nearly 180 died. PAF7740

Old World and the New: in them, migrants from Britain, mainland Europe, Scandinavia and Russia sought a better life, escaping poverty, war, famine, over-population and persecution.

In 1815 it could take a month to cross the Atlantic. There was no timetable because the duration and the route were entirely dependent on prevailing conditions. Most migrants

also had to take with them everything necessary for the journey, including food. Fires were commonplace on wooden-hulled sailing vessels, due mainly to passengers cooking their own meals. Exploitation was rife. Emigrants waiting to leave from British ports were met by 'runners' who acted as middlemen between them and passage-brokers. Runners were notorious for cheating emigrants over luggage, currency exchange and the purchase of provisions for the voyage. Eventually the Passenger Act of 1855 required runners to be registered and to wear an official badge. In 1848 the British government published a report on emigration which revealed that, in the previous year, 89,738 fare-paying passengers had embarked for Canada but 17,465 had died either on the voyage or in quarantine on arrival.

The gradual introduction of steamships from the 1830s began to improve conditions. By 1900 it took just seven days to travel from Liverpool to New York: by then migrants could enjoy set meals and had access to washing facilities on board.

Sea War: 1588 to 1815

T HE MUSEUM has extraordinary resources which help to tell the story of the Royal Navy and naval conflict, from the time of the Spanish Armada in 1588 to the end of the Second World War. Focusing here on the seventeenth and eighteenth centuries, naval wars were fought for three main reasons: to defend Britain against invasion, to protect and expand trade, and to gain territory overseas. For instance, during the three wars fought against the Dutch between the 1650s and the 1670s, the Navy was at the cutting edge of London's ambitions to compete with Amsterdam for the profits of seaborne trade.

The Seven Years War (1756–63) saw the Navy play a key role in taking Canada from the French and securing Britain's position in the Caribbean. The French Revolutionary and Napoleonic Wars, however, placed the Navy at the heart of a bitter struggle for national survival. Throughout this period, therefore, conflict placed extensive demands upon it. The great fleet actions are famous, with their lines of wooden warships engaged in savage duels of close-range gunnery: but the era was also one of amphibious landings, marauding privateers and gruelling blockades of enemy coastlines.

The riches of our collections – from flags flown in action and letters written by Nelson, to cannons raised from the seabed and dramatic paintings of the many battles – capture the realities of naval warfare. A variety of objects, be they spectacular gifts presented to naval officers or humble commemorative ceramics, also show the impact that war at sea could have on the lives of men and women at home.

The Battle of Trafalgar, 21 October 1805, by Joseph Mallord William Turner, 1822–24, with Nelson's *Victory* in the centre. Greenwich Hospital Collection. BHC0565

Building Warships

ACROSS THE CENTURIES, warships have ranked among the most complex objects created by human hand. They have taken many forms, from Nelson's 'wooden walls' to the giant steel battleships that clashed during the First World War. The Museum's collections tell the story of how these vessels were constructed – and of the people who built them – from the seventeenth to the twentieth centuries.

For the first half of this period, the story is dominated by the Royal Dockyards at Deptford, Woolwich, Chatham, Sheerness, Portsmouth and Plymouth. These were the greatest industrial sites of the age, employing thousands of skilled workers including carpenters, shipwrights, sailmakers and ropemakers. Raw materials poured through their gates, not least the thousands of oak trees required to build a single ship of the line.

The nineteenth century brought forces that revolutionized both the traditional practices of naval shipbuilding and the nature of conflict at sea. By the time of the Crimean War (1853–56), some Royal Naval warships were powered by paddle wheels or propellers, in addition to sails, and the pace of change rapidly accelerated. Iron hulls, breech-loading guns, explosive shells and torpedoes appeared within a few decades, and by the end of the century a battleship could become obsolete while still under construction. Two world wars further transformed the capabilities of warships and saw the rise of wholly new types of vessel, such as the aircraft carrier and the submarine.

From eighteenth-century craftsmanship to Victorian invention, and from the toil of the shipyard to the symbolism of the ship launch, our collections reveal the many faces of the warship.

A contemporary full-hull model of the 32-gun frigate *Amazon*, a warship built on the River Thames at Rotherhithe during the 1770s. SLR0315

Sea War: 1815 to Now

NELSON'S VICTORY at the Battle of Trafalgar in 1805 left Britain with an unrivalled command of the oceans for more than a century. Conflict was far from suspended, however. The nineteenth century saw the Royal Navy highly active in the campaign to end slavery, as well as fighting around the world to promote or defend the interests of Britain's growing empire. By 1900 tensions within Europe were again mounting and a fierce naval arms race had broken out between Britain and Germany.

The war that followed (1914–18) made unprecedented demands on the Navy but, to some extent, these have been overshadowed by the terrible slaughter of the trenches and debates surrounding the controversial naval Battle of Jutland in 1916. The wider reality is that Britain's war effort depended on supplies of food and raw materials imported by merchant vessels: if the Navy had failed to defend this lifeline against German submarines, then national defeat and starvation might have followed. During the Second World War (1939–45), the scale of the Navy's commitments increased still further. The war at sea stretched from the Pacific to the Arctic, and from a second brutal contest with German U-boats to the Normandy landings on D-Day. Boosted by hundreds of thousands of volunteers and conscripts, this 'People's War' was fought by a people's navy, supported by colossal industrial effort at home.

Since 1945, the Royal Navy's role in conflict has continued, from Korea to the Falkland Islands, Iraq, Afghanistan and Libya. The two centuries since Trafalgar have, therefore, seen the realities of naval warfare dramatically transformed: canvas and cutlasses have been replaced by nuclear power and guided missiles.

Withdrawal from Dunkirk, June 1940,
by Richard Ernst Eurich, 1940. One of the artist's best known early works painted for the War Artists Advisory Committee. BHC0672

Experiencing Conflict

T HE COLLECTIONS of the Museum paint a vivid picture of how real people – from lower-deck sailors to celebrated admirals – have experienced the ordeals of conflict. For instance, first-hand accounts reveal the horrors of warfare during the age of sail and the courage displayed by crews from many nations. Frequently fought at close range, or hand-to-hand, battle in this era exposed naval personnel to a range of hazards.

In this wooden world, cannon shot could sweep the decks of a ship, upturning gun carriages and sending showers of lethal splinters in every direction: men were hit by falling debris and the danger of fire always threatened. The dress coat worn by Nelson at the Battle of Trafalgar powerfully conveys these perils: the musket ball that mortally wounded him left a hole in the fabric on the left shoulder. Other voices describe the sufferings endured by the injured, with surgery carried out in primitive conditions and without anaesthetics or effective antiseptics.

As weapons and vessels changed, battle also brought new fears. The power of long-range gunnery could destroy a mighty warship in an instant – the fate that befell HMS *Hood* in 1941 – and men who worked deep below the waterline in engine rooms or magazines knew that a torpedo strike would leave them with little chance of escape.

One adversary remained the same across time: the weather. Sailors have always faced more than human violence, be it in the deadly gale that blew up after Trafalgar, or the Atlantic and Arctic storms endured by convoy escorts and merchant vessels during the Second World War. Our collections also show the bonds that linked ship and shore during conflict, from letters greeting loved ones at home to poignant mourning jewellery commemorating those who would never return.

ABOVE: *Rear-Admiral Sir Horatio Nelson*, by Lemuel Francis Abbott, 1799. Greenwich Hospital Collection. BHC2889

OPPOSITE: **The undress uniform coat** worn by Nelson when he was fatally wounded during the Battle of Trafalgar in 1805. Greenwich Hospital Collection. UNI0024

OVERLEAF: **Detail from a Chinese export vase**, *c*.1800, given to Nelson by Queen Maria-Carolina of Naples. AAAE4723

Merchant Adventurers

Britain's history has been shaped by its relationship with the sea. The possibilities and profits offered by maritime trade were particularly important in defining the country's development as a global power. Commercial contacts with continental neighbours were well established by the fifteenth century, with traders from the British Isles involved in the commerce of the North Sea, the Baltic and the Mediterranean. But merchants soon began to look further afield: early English voyages across the Atlantic were made to expand fishing, to challenge the Spanish hold on Central and South America, and to establish colonies further north in Virginia, New England and the Caribbean.

The careers of individual seafarers reflected England's (and after 1707, Britain's) rising worldwide ambitions to compete overseas with continental rivals. In 1577–80, Francis Drake sailed round the world and returned with a cargo of Asian spices as well as captured Spanish treasure. James Lancaster soon followed: in 1591 he accompanied the first English trading voyage to the East Indies. Although it was a commercial failure, the expedition foreshadowed one of the most important financial elements in Britain's later global dominance: trade with Asia.

By the mid-seventeenth century, overseas trade was tightly controlled by the Navigation Acts, a series of laws that restricted the use of foreign shipping for British colonial trade. Merchant enterprise was encouraged and regulated by royal charters, which gave monopoly trading rights – and the profits from it – to groups of investors trading with particular regions. Muscovy and Levant Companies traded, respectively, with Russia and Turkey, while the Royal African Company, the Hudson's Bay Company and the South Sea Company were all involved in Atlantic trade. In 1600, Elizabeth I awarded a royal charter to the East India Company, giving it a monopoly on all English trade east of the Cape of Good Hope.

ABOVE AND OPPOSITE:
The South Sea Company Coat of Arms, carved by Robert Jones, 1711–12. The Company held the monopoly on British trade with Spain's colonies in South America: the 'South Seas' then meant the south Atlantic and south Pacific. HRA0043

OVERLEAF: **British & North American Royal Mail Steam Ship 'Persia'**, engineering drawing by David Kirkaldy, 1856. DKY0001

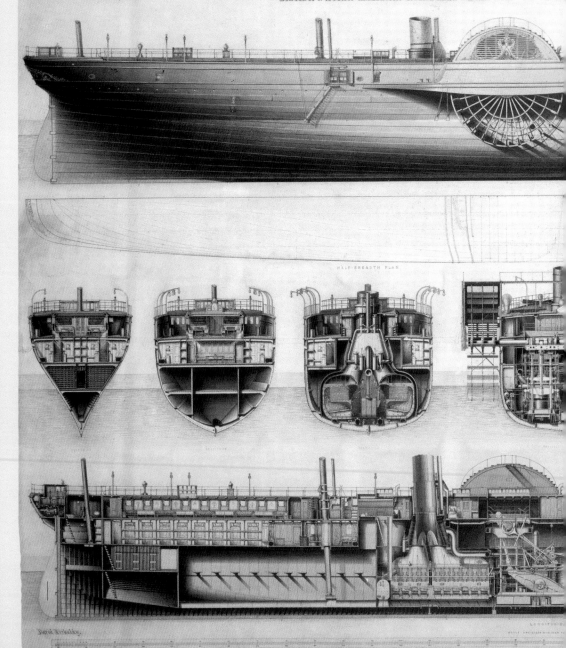

BRITISH & NORTH AMERICAN ROYAL MAIL STEAM SHIP "PER

CONSTRUCTED BY MESS^{RS} R. NAPIER & SONS, GLASGOW.

Global Networks

I N 1700, MOST BRITISH OVERSEAS TRADE – in volume and value – was still conducted with Europe. Over the next hundred years, Britain's commercial reach and ambitions expanded considerably, becoming more 'global' in the process.

Increasing numbers of ships sailed the transatlantic route to North America, where a network of colonies had been established following the permanent settlement of Virginia in 1607. With the seizure of Jamaica from Spain in 1655, the Caribbean also became a key source of wealth. These riches were based on plantation economies, which relied on the unpaid mass labour of enslaved Africans to produce sugar, tobacco and other crops for consumers in Europe. The transatlantic slave trade, in which Britain was a major participant, supplied American and Caribbean colonies with millions of Africans. Their bondage was paid for in Africa with British-made goods like firearms, metal wares and alcohol. This trade was only abolished in 1807, when an Act of Parliament made it illegal for British subjects to trade in slaves. The institution of slavery was outlawed throughout the British Empire in 1833–34.

At the same time, Britain increasingly dominated European trade with Asia. The East India Company, with its monopoly on British trade to the region, became one of the most powerful and influential commercial organizations in the world. Between 1600 and 1833, ships sailing under Company colours made about 4,600 voyages from London to Asia. These ships, called Indiamen, brought back goods like Indian textiles and Chinese tea that were in huge demand in Europe.

LEFT: **Shipping Sugar**, hand-coloured etching after William Clark, 1823. Sugar was grown by enslaved Africans on Caribbean and American plantations. Between 1750 and 1820, it was Britain's largest single import. PAH3019

OVERLEAF: **The Mast House and Brunswick Dock at Blackwall**, by William Daniell, c.1803. The view looks down the Thames towards Woolwich. The tip of Greenwich Marshes (Blackwall Point) is on the right. Green Blackwall Collection. BHC1867

Facilitating Commerce

By 1815, British overseas trade went hand-in-hand with Britain's global empire. New markets were exploited, and Britain's volume and share of world trade continued to grow throughout the nineteenth century. This seaborne economic success relied on a sophisticated domestic infrastructure of port facilities, dock systems and financial services.

While the importance of Britain's Atlantic trade led to the development of ports such as Bristol, Liverpool and Glasgow, London was always the largest and most significant. It accounted for nearly half of customs revenues in the late sixteenth century: by the early nineteenth century it was the world's largest port and the centre

of international finance. From the 1790s on a series of enclosed dock systems was built, increasing efficiency in the loading, unloading and secure storage of goods.

London's commercial success relied on highly developed shipbuilding and repairing facilities, which underpinned a global merchant fleet operation and employed thousands of people. For example, the Brunswick Dock was built in the mid-1790s by John Perry, adjacent to his shipyard at Blackwall, which by that time was the world's largest merchant yard and also built naval vessels on contract. The history of the Blackwall site reflected the vital importance of maritime trade to Britain in the period. In the 1820s a managing interest passed to Perry's son-in-law, George Green. His son, Richard, made it famous as the home of 'Blackwall frigates', the last development of large Indiamen, and of Green's Blackwall line, which traded to both India and Australia. Ship repairing on the site only ended in 1980.

Commercial Consolidation

B Y THE MID-NINETEENTH CENTURY, a maritime technological revolution – the development of iron shipbuilding and steam propulsion – had given Britain a powerful economic advantage over its commercial rivals. Steamships were beginning to replace sailing vessels, introducing regular and increasingly rapid communication with every corner of the globe. In this they were aided by advances in land-based technology. In 1869 Europe and Asia were brought 3,000 miles closer together by the opening of the Suez Canal. This was crucial for trade: by 1900 India consumed almost one fifth of British exports, and the canal also connected Europe with other areas of vital commercial and political interest to Britain.

Between 1890 and 1914, Britain's merchant shipping carried up to 60 per cent of the world's trade and built two-thirds of its ships. While twentieth-century events ended that

BELOW:
A full-hull builder's model
of the *Nonsuch*, *c*.1906.
Ships like this turret-deck
general cargo vessel plied
the route through the Suez
Canal. SLR0083

supremacy, the sea remains vital to Britain's economy: ships still carry over 90 per cent of the country's trade – in food, raw materials and manufactured goods.

Patterns of British overseas trade, first created by individual merchants and monopoly trading companies, endured and developed through imperial ties and technological innovations. Trade brought wealth but commercial dominance created powerful forces whose consequences influenced many other areas of British life. The insatiable demand for resources and markets encouraged greater exploration of the world's oceans. Commercial and business links also led to transoceanic migration from the British Isles on a vast scale. In turn, the defence of trading stations and shipping routes lay at the root of many of the conflicts in which Britain was involved over the centuries. Merchant shipping relied on naval protection and, apart from defending Britain from foreign invasion, protecting trade was the Royal Navy's most important role.

OVERLEAF: **Part of the First World War memorial stained-glass 'half-dome'**, from the Baltic Exchange (the main London shipping exchange), 1922, designed by John Dudley Forsyth. The Exchange was demolished after severe damage by a terrorist bomb in 1992 but much of the memorial glass was restored and presented to the Museum by Swiss Re, who redeveloped the site. ZBA4360.1

OVERLEAF PAGES 38–39:
An Interesting scene on board an East Indiaman, showing the Effects of a heavy lurch, after dinner, coloured etching by George Cruikshank, 1818. PAG8632

VICTORY

The Great British Seaside

AS AN ISLAND NATION with such a diverse coastline, it is unsurprising that the British have a long fascination with 'the seaside'. Since the eighteenth century many British coastal towns have become synonymous with rest, recuperation and leisure. Seaside resorts were put on the map when George, Prince of Wales, (later Prince Regent and, from 1820, George IV), built the Royal Pavilion at Brighton as his own spectacular sea-view residence. Royal patronage of other resorts led to them adding 'Regis' to their names, for status: Melcombe Regis ('King's Melcombe'), frequented by George III, is an example.

The genteel world of the Regency coastal retreat was transformed by the Victorians. The expanding railway network, industrialization and urbanization created 'seaside resort' towns and the 'traditional' summer holidays they still offer. By the late nineteenth century, the largely working-class holiday market in such resorts had many attractions, including pleasure palaces, piers and promenades. All the traditions of seaside family fun were invented by the Victorians: donkey rides, Punch and Judy, buckets and spades, sandcastles, boats trips and candy floss.

Between the two World Wars there was a huge rise in families with time and the money to take seaside holidays, and this had far-reaching consequences for the towns involved. Local authorities began running their resorts along commercial lines and appealing to new markets. Modernist attractions like the De La Warr Pavilion at Bexhill-on-Sea became chic, stylish destinations, but the British seaside was eventually to lose its lustre and popularity to foreign package holidays. Today, however, seaside resorts are making a comeback typified by the Midland Hotel at Morecambe: in 2008, following years of neglect, it opened its splendid Art-Deco doors again, following a lengthy refurbishment.

Scarborough, a London and North Eastern Railway poster designed by William Barribal, c.1930, advertising the fashionable attractions of this well-known Yorkshire seaside town.

Yachting for Sport and Recreation

PEOPLE HAVE BEEN USING the wind to sail vessels for millennia, but the racing of sailing craft is thought to have started in the Netherlands during the seventeenth century. In the 1660s Charles II imported it to England as a royal sport, where custom-built racing 'yachts' began to emerge. Yachting is usually associated with affluent lifestyles and for good reason: competitive sailing can be an expensive business.

There are a number of high-profile races in the yachting calendar like Australia's Sydney to Hobart Yacht Race or, nearer to home, the Fastnet Race. The greatest contest of all is for the America's Cup, first held in 1851 and today the oldest active trophy event in competitive sport. The inaugural race was between the New York Yacht Club, representing the USA, and the Royal Yacht Squadron of Great Britain. The winner was the New York yacht, *America*, which gave its name to the trophy. Thereafter, the USA won every America's Cup series until 1983, when it was beaten by the Royal Perth Yacht Club's *Australia II*, ending the longest winning streak in the history of sport.

Yachting is also a lifestyle and in recent decades it has become as much a pastime as a sport. Marinas have proliferated around Britain, holding sailing and powered boats of every size and description. Yachts are manufactured as mass-produced items for a mass-market, and modern technology has made them easier to handle and to navigate. At the top of the range, large motor yachts continue to be built for a wealthy and exclusive clientele. In 1900 Gordon Bennett's steam yacht *Lysistrata* included enough room for his dairy cow: now some luxury motor yachts can accommodate several cars in their holds.

ABOVE: **Dutch yachts racing**, by Andries van Eertvelt. A dramatic early racing, *c.*1635. Macpherson Collection. BHC0741

OVERLEAF: *HMY* Britannia *Racing the Yacht* Westward
in the Solent, by Norman Wilkinson, 1935. *Britannia*
was King George V's own racing yacht and was scuttled,
as he wished, after his death in 1935. BHC3750

Norman Wilkinson

Cruise Ships

T HE IDEA OF TRAVELLING BY SEA for sheer enjoyment began as early as 1836 when Arthur Anderson, who was to become a founder of the shipping line P&O, floated the idea in *The Shetland Journal*. At the time he was not a ship operator and had no vessels, but, perhaps for the first time, he did give people the idea of sea travel purely for pleasure. P&O started cruising as a dedicated business in 1904, around fifteen years after Orient Line.

To begin with destinations were modest: trips around the British coast, the Norwegian fjords, the Mediterranean and occasionally further afield. By 1939, however, there was an enormous choice of cruise itineraries, from Acapulco to Zanzibar. For those on limited budgets some companies offered the inducement of an upgrade from 'second-class' to the new classification of 'tourist-class'. Before the term became denigrated to mean what it was originally supposed to replace, it literally referred to passengers who had the time to tour.

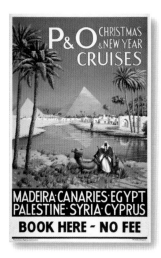

Low-cost air travel and holidays overseas led to a downturn in the cruise-ship business in the 1970s and 80s. More recently all that has changed and it is now a multi-billion-dollar global business, growing year-on-year. Companies like Carnival Cruise Line and Royal Caribbean have huge modern fleets, with each new ship frequently larger than its predecessor. Cunard Line's *Queen Mary 2*, at 1,132 feet in length and of 151,400 tons gross, boasts facilities including an art gallery, planetarium and a branch of Harrods. The more traditional cruise experience also continues to flourish in the hands of specialist operators.

ABOVE: **P&O Cruises poster** *c.*1936. ZBA0573

OPPOSITE: **The Swedish America Line ship *Kungsholm*** at anchor in Geirangerfjord, Norway, *c.*1935, image taken by the Marine Photo Service. P83842

The Wave

THE 'VOYAGERS' GALLERY introduces visitors to the National Maritime Museum's collections, the way in which the sea surrounds us, how the sea has shaped people's lives and the course of British history and Britain's character today. Audio-visual sequences projected onto a large 'wave' structure illustrate key themes of the maritime story: exploration, conflict, technology, navigation, trade and leisure, as well as the power and nature of the sea. The images show the sea as a place of beauty and a source of inspiration, while also being potentially dangerous and a cause of separation. They provide a preview of some of the objects and documents which are either on display throughout the Museum or accessible in the archive. They also give a sense of the courage, work, ingenuity, skill and imagination of the people who made Britain such a richly varied maritime nation.

Britain's relationship with the sea produced wealth and power, though sometimes at a terrible human cost. At the local level, it created communities in ports and on ships and, more widely, interactions and cultural exchange on an international scale. It led to mass movements of people – both free and forced – around the globe. Over centuries, these movements helped to create our multicultural society and spread the use of the English language throughout the world.

The Museum tells the story of this multifaceted engagement with the sea. It is one that continues and is relevant to us all today: it helps explain the voyages we have all taken to arrive here – and where we may be heading. We need to be aware that what happens at sea now will affect the future for everyone.

A local surf-boat landing European passengers on the beach at Madras, watercolour by unknown artist, *c*.1800. PAD1842

People Stories

THE SHOWCASES in the 'Voyagers' gallery present stories of people during episodes in their lives which were shaped by their connections with the sea. The characters depicted convey a range of emotions: anticipation, love, sadness, aggression, pride and joy. This provides a way of linking people across time and space. Because history is a tapestry of many lives, traditional heroes are mixed up with individuals who did not achieve such fame.

These are examples from each of the sections. *Anticipation*: whale-ship captain William Brookes roamed the Pacific on voyages lasting for years, searching for whales, unable to go home until his ship was full of oil. *Love*: John Treleaven and June Kellett fell in love but his naval career meant they were often apart, and John died tragically in a submarine accident a year and a day after their wedding. *Sadness*: Lord Nelson's lover, Emma Hamilton was so devastated by his death that she kept the bullet-holed coat that he wore at the Battle of Trafalgar on her bed. *Aggression*: Admiral David Beatty demanded the unconditional surrender of the German Navy at the end of the First World War. *Pride*: Katharine Furse set up the Wrens (the Women's Royal Naval Service) and was proud of their work. *Joy*: T. P. Cooke's theatrical song-and-dance roles celebrated the brave and romantic image of the sailor.

The diversity of life experiences connected to the sea is matched by the range of exhibits. These are items that the characters owned, used or created, and which represent them, the places where they went and their relationships with other people. They illustrate aspects of what made them human and what the sea meant to them.

Big Ben the Bargee,
by Bernard Hailstone, 1943.
Painted at Hull during the Second
World War for the War Artists
Advisory Committee. BHC3146

Where History Begins

Peter Butchard started performing seaside Punch and Judy shows in the 1950s and became so well known that letters simply addressed to 'Mr Punch, Broadstairs' would reach him. He loved the work so much that he continued until he was 90. His collection of puppets, photographs and letters of appreciation from children who watched the shows are now in the Museum's collections and archive. Another person whose possessions feature in the Joy section of the 'Voyagers' gallery is Tracy Edwards, who won the Whitbread Round the World Yacht Race in 1990, the first time that a yacht crewed entirely by women had competed.

ABOVE: **Glove puppet of Mr Punch's wife, Judy**, belonging to puppeteer Peter Butchard. ZBA2300

RIGHT: **Peter Butchard (1909–2009)**, Punch and Judy man in performance. X2001.038 (2)

Things from our own lifetimes often seem too familiar to be worth keeping but they will seem strange to future generations: as with objects from earlier ages, they will reveal what life could be like at different times, in different places and for different social groups. Museums preserve and provide access to artefacts and records so that the past can be understood by piecing together its surviving fragments. They tell us more than the bare facts of history, not only recording what happened but also giving insights into what it meant for people at the time, and the diversity of human experience.

Collections relating to all the characters featured in the 'Voyagers' gallery are housed in the Museum alongside many thousands more, including those of explorers and entertainers, mutineers and heroes, royalty and ordinary seamen, scientists and artists, emigrants, traders, whalers and workers. This provides a unique resource for finding out how the sea influenced the lives of people in the past and for discovering your own maritime connections. It is open for everyone to enjoy.

RMS *Titanic*

Titanic STRUCK AN ICEBERG at 11.40 p.m. on the night of 14 April 1912, sinking at 2.20 a.m. on the 15th with the loss of 1,517 passengers and crew. This is not the worst maritime disaster – that dubious distinction belongs to the estimated 9,000 lives lost when the MV *Wilhelm Gustloff* was torpedoed by a Russian submarine in 1945 – but it is arguably the most famous.

BELOW: **2nd-Class dinner menu from RMS** *Titanic*, 14 April 1912. LMQ/1/12/2

The menu *(right)* belonged to nine-year-old Roberta Josephine 'Bertha' Watts, who was travelling with her mother, Elizabeth, to join her architect father in Portland, Oregon. There was heavy loss of life among the second-class passengers (more than half died) but Bertha and Elizabeth were among those rescued by the *Carpathia*. Bertha (by then Mrs Marshall) presented the menu to Walter Lord in the early 1950s, when he was doing research for his book, *A Night to Remember* (1955), which reinvigorated interest in the loss of the *Titanic*. The menu came to the Museum as part of the Lord-MacQuitty bequest in 2002.

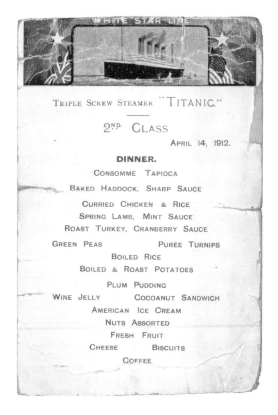

Lord collaborated with the producer William MacQuitty on the 1958 British film of the same title, directed by Roy Ward Baker and starring Kenneth More. Since 1912 the disaster has inspired over twenty films, including James Cameron's 1997 blockbuster, *Titanic*. There have also been numerous books, poems, radio plays and songs, including a black-American folksong celebrating the fictional survival of a stoker who swam to shore after the sinking.

There will undoubtedly be more, for the myth of the *Titanic* has enduring fascination: the supposedly unsinkable ship, lost on its

OPPOSITE: *Titanic* **sinking bow first in the early morning of 15 April 1912**, watercolour by W. Pearson. PAH5224

maiden voyage, has become a symbol of human arrogance, folly, fortitude, selfishness and self-sacrifice, and of a complacently stratified society about to meet its end in the even greater tragedy of the First World War.

The Painter and Poedua

T HE SWISS-BORN ARTIST John Webber (1751–93) accompanied James Cook's third voyage of Pacific exploration (1776–80). Directed to 'diligently employ himself in making Drawings … of such places … that may be worthy of notice', Webber made many fine studies of Pacific people.

Cook knew Poedua, the daughter of the chief of Raiatea, from his second voyage (1772–75), describing her as 'a pretty brown girl at whose Shrine … many pretty things were offered by her numerous Votarists'. Webber sketched her in the ship's cabin in 1777, this finished version being painted later in England and exhibited at the Royal Academy in 1785; two others are known, but not the original sketch.

The portrait has been described as having the 'mood of serious eroticism' that, from the first, pervaded European representations of the Pacific in art and literature. Poedua is the forerunner of Herman Melville's island beauty, Fayaway (in *Typee*, 1846), Pierre Loti's Rarahu (in *The Marriage of Loti*, 1880), R.L. Stevenson's Uma (in *The Beach of Falesá*, 1892); also of figures in Paul Gauguin's paintings of Polynesia and the Rodgers and Hammerstein musical, *South Pacific* (1949). Although Webber's image gives

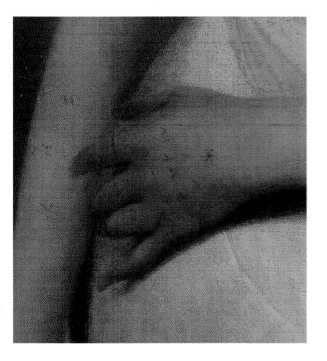

ABOVE: **Detail from *Poedua*** showing tattooing on her hand and arms. The word 'tattoo' entered the English language from the Polynesian 'tatau' after Cook's voyages.

Poedua an air of sexual invitation, she was, in fact, being held hostage (with others) to bring about the return of two deserters when the sketch was made. Alongside the ship, wrote Charles Clerke, captain of *Discovery*, 'we had a most numerous Congregation of Women … cutting their Heads with Sharks Teeth and lamenting the Fate of the Prisoners.'

A Seaman's 'Journal': Truth or Fiction?

ABOVE: *Patty Awakening Penrose*, by William Bird (1772–1819), and OPPOSITE: *Penrose greets Ayasharra and Yalutta*, by Nicholas Pocock (1740–1821), two watercolours from the manuscript of *The Journal of Llewellin Penrose, Seaman*, by William Williams. LIT/11

THE WATERCOLOURS shown here are two of 37 intended for, but eventually not engraved in, the published version of William Williams' *Journal of Llewellin Penrose, Seaman.* This purports to be the memoirs of a sailor shipwrecked in the Caribbean, where he lived for 27 years among the 'Indians'. Williams (1727–91) was born in Bristol and went to sea as a teenager. Around 1745 he travelled to the Caribbean to accomplish his 'wish to be a painter'. He may have spent a year among the Rama people of Nicaragua, for *Penrose* contains much accurate local detail. How much is autobiographical, though, is debatable: more obvious influences are popular colonial romances such as *Inkle and Yarico* (1711) and Daniel Defoe's *Robinson Crusoe* (1719).

The *Journal* was written while Williams worked as an artist in America (1747–76) and is claimed to be the first novel written there. He returned to England in 1776 and on his death the manuscript passed to his benefactor, Thomas Eagles. It was unsympathetically edited for publication by Eagles, who commissioned illustrations from Nicholas Pocock and Edward Bird, although most are by Eagles' son, the Rev. John Eagles. A competent watercolourist, the Rev. Eagles saw the book through publication in 1815, after his father's death. Sir Walter Scott thought it overlong, but Lord Byron was so enraptured that he read it at a single sitting and the *Critical Review* admired its 'moral tendency'. The Museum purchased the manuscript, with the illustrations, in 2006 with the support of the Macpherson Endowment Fund of the Society for Nautical Research.

A Terminal View

T HROUGHOUT THE TWENTIETH CENTURY the sea continued to inspire leading British artists, including the painter John Wonnacott (born 1940). Yet, interestingly, his impressive *Winter Afternoon: Container Ships off Felixstowe, 1993–94* was painted while Britain's identity as a maritime nation was generally on the decline, owing to the dramatic changes brought by the globalization of modern industry, maritime communities, shipping and travel. Indeed, the vast container port of Felixstowe itself and the panoramic, mechanized portrayal of its Trinity Terminal in Wonnacott's painting, effectively illustrate this very alienation of the sea as an arena of trade from general modern consciousness.

The painter has given the sky the heroic lead in this dramatic composition. 'I paint as I live', writes Wonnacott, 'dominated by the anarchic splendours of the East Anglian sky. Sky provides the wild card in my painting. It floods each landscape with particular atmospheric light while fighting the elaborate formal plotting of my geometry.'

Bands of white clouds draw the spectator's gaze deep into the vast picture space. From the elevated viewpoint above the roofs of the industrial buildings of the port, competing diagonals lead the eye beyond the docked container vessels onto the North Sea. No human activity catches the attention: with the exception of a lone, tiny figure on the left, the scene appears empty and the industrial processes of a modern port are fractured into geometrical shapes.

The painting was commissioned by the Museum in 1993 and kindly facilitated by the Port of Felixstowe. Regrettably, they were disappointed with it for just the reasons the Museum considered it a success in representing, not a romantic celebration of an undoubtedly critical maritime industry but its disorienting scale and isolation, on the perimeter of general public awareness.

LEFT: **Winter Afternoon: Container Ships off Felixstowe, 1993–94**, by John Wonnacott. BHC4249

OVERLEAF: **Table clock** (detail), a magnificent example of the Renaissance clockmaker's art made by Caspar Buschman and Johann Reinhold in Augsburg, 1486. ZAA0011

Exploring the World

W HAT DOES IT MEAN to explore? For thousands of years, curiosity and a need to find new resources have encouraged people to sail beyond their known worlds. Europeans' desire to explore the oceans grew rapidly from the fifteenth century, as competing powers looked for better trade routes: when Columbus 'discovered' the Americas in 1492 he was trying to reach the riches of Asia. The desire to dominate the trade in spices such as pepper, and later other commodities like tea and textiles, continued to play a major part in European exploration. The search for new ways to reach Asia was a stimulus for voyages to both the Pacific and the Arctic. However, by 1900, Europeans had explored and charted all the world's oceans. They were helped by new technologies and improvements in navigation and cartography, but also often enlisted local knowledge to help. Only the polar ice proved frustratingly difficult to penetrate and scientists

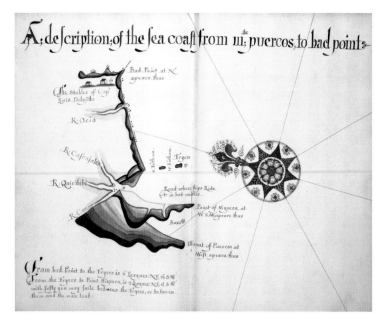

LEFT: *A description of the sea coast from Mta. Puercos to Bad Point*, by William Hack, 1685, from the 'pirate's atlas' of the Pacific coast of South America, copied from sailing directions captured from the Spanish ship *Rosario* by Captain Bartholomew Sharpe in 1681. Sharpe was acquitted of piracy after giving a copy of the manuscript, which showed the Spanish silver mines, to Charles II. This copy was presented to James II. P/33(44)

OPPOSITE: **World map on vellum**, by Nicholas Desliens, 1567. This early French view of the world labels what is now called the North Atlantic Ocean as the 'Sea of France'. G201:1/51

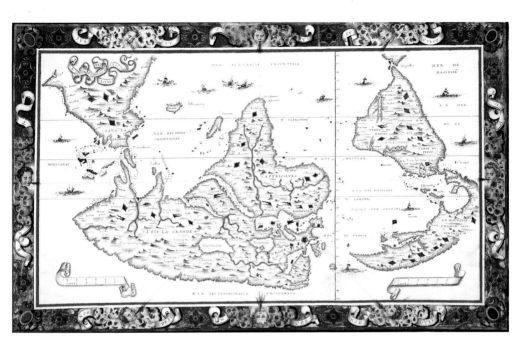

OVERLEAF: **Chart on vellum of the seas around Europe and North Africa**, by Vesconte Maggiolo, 1548. Showing the Baltic Sea in blue and the Red Sea in red, it is exuberantly decorated with symbols for kingdoms and towns. A little-explored world, with strange and mythical beasts, lies beyond the Atlas Mountains. G230:1/4

OVERLEAF, PAGES 68–69: **An engraved fool's map of the world**, *c.*1590. The map is based on one of 1587 by Ortelius, with classical quotations praising man's discovery and mastery of the world. By putting a jester's hood on the map, its anonymous engraver satirizes the vanity of this view and proclaims that 'the stupidity of man is limitless'. G201:1/43

were still debating whether Antarctica was one continent or two in the mid-twentieth century.

Today, exploration continues, as we try to learn more about our world and about the planets beyond it. Although the oceans cover much of the Earth, they are relatively unexplored. Scientists are now trying to understand the life, resources and processes beneath their surface, as they are crucial to the way in which our planet functions. They influence our climate and provide essential resources, such as food, energy and minerals. Population growth, marine pollution and over-exploitation are all threatening the health of the oceans, while other man-made environmental change is beginning to affect them in ways that we do not yet fully understand.

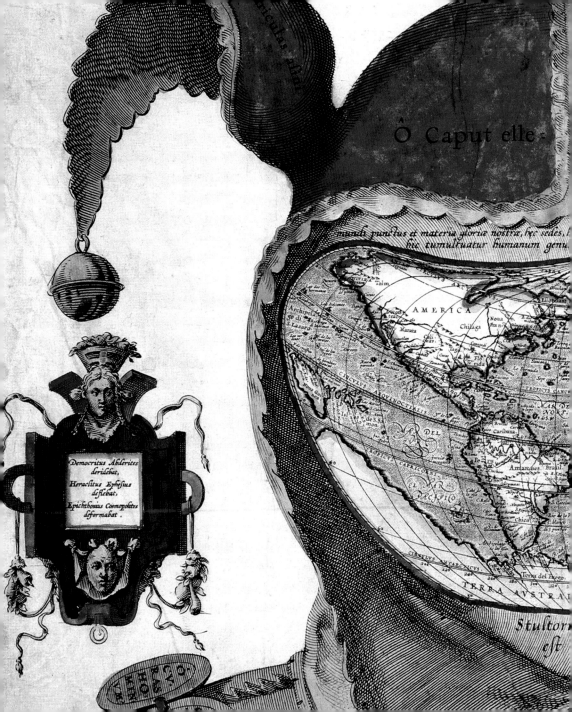

Ô Caput elle-

mundi punctus et materia gloriæ nostræ, hæc sedes,
hic tumultuatur humanum genus

O
Caput elle-

Democritus Abderites
deridebat,
Heraclitus Ephesius
deflebat,
Epichthonius Cosmopolites
deformabat.

Stultor
est

AMERICA

Discovery and Empire

TRADE – AND THE CONTROL OF IT through colonization – fuelled early European discovery. Different nations thus competed to discover new lands. Exploration of the Pacific was stimulated by the desire to find the fastest routes to Asia, while early understanding of the globe also led Europeans to believe in the existence of an undiscovered 'Southern Continent' which might be a source of wealth for the first to find it.

Europe saw an Age of Enlightenment in the late-seventeenth and eighteenth centuries, and voyages often had new scientific purposes. Captain James Cook's, between 1768 and 1780, included work in astronomy, natural history, geography and the charting of the Pacific. Cook and his men encountered groups of indigenous people hitherto unknown to most Europeans. Their exchanges and interactions were to have profound effects for both.

Scientific exploration continued to be important in the nineteenth century. Darwin's voyage in the *Beagle*, as part of a

ABOVE: **The badge of a Knight Commander of the Royal Hanovarian Guelphic Order**, a relic of Sir John Franklin's last expedition (1845–48). Awarded to him in 1836, it was recovered from the Inuit at Repulse Bay in 1854 by the Rae Expedition. AAA2079

LEFT: **Marine timekeeper K3**, made by Larcum Kendall, 1774. Issued to Captain James Cook on his third voyage of discovery in 1776. ZAA0111

Royal Naval charting expedition (1831–36), provided the observations from which he developed his groundbreaking theory of evolution, and in doing so forever changed the way that we see the world. Other important voyages of exploration included that of HMS *Challenger* in 1872–76, a mammoth 68,890-mile trip that attempted to investigate life beneath the sea's surface. Using a raft of new technologies, it has sometimes been seen as the birth of oceanography.

Scientific discovery did not happen in a vacuum, however. Voyages of exploration were often sponsored by government bodies, such as the Admiralty, and the knowledge gathered was also used to serve national interests: science, exploration and empire were often closely linked.

BELOW: *Resolution* and *Adventure* in **Matavai Bay, Tahiti**, on Cook's second Pacific voyage, 1772–74, as painted in 1776 by William Hodges, official artist on the expedition. Ministry of Defence Art Collection. BHC1932

The Challenge of the Poles

THE POLAR REGIONS were important areas for exploration in the ninteenth and twentieth centuries. The search for the fabled North-West Passage, which was thought to link the Atlantic and the Pacific, had begun in the sixteenth century. Initially, everyone hoped that the Passage might provide a faster sea route to Asia but it slowly became clear that any such route was commercially impracticable. In the 1840s it was the quest for national glory through discovery that drove Sir John Franklin's search for it: he and his crew – 129 men – all died. In the 1870s the Royal Navy abandoned Arctic exploration as profitless, and it was the Norwegian, Roald Amundsen, who first sailed through the Passage in 1904–06.

British naval and merchant seamen nevertheless played leading roles in the great age of Antarctic exploration, from the 1890s to the First World War. Captain Scott RN reached within 100 miles of the South Pole in 1901 but in 1912 his small party died on their return, having being beaten to the Pole by Amundsen. In 1914–16 Ernest Shackleton's trans-Antarctic expedition became a triumph of survival without even reaching the coast.

With the exception of Antarctica, European explorers have rarely ventured into unpeopled lands. The shot pouch shown here encapsulates the kind of interaction that occurred during the course of their voyages. Collected on one of the Royal Navy's overland expeditions to the Arctic, it was probably made by a talented craftswoman of mixed European and native descent, who skilfully crafted from it animal skin and porcupine quills. Without the skills of local people, Europeans would have found 'discovery' very difficult indeed.

PREVIOUS: *The War-Boats of the Island of Otaheite* [Tahiti] *and the Society Islands, with a View of Part of the Harbour of Ohaneneno* [Haamanino], *in the Island of Ulietea* [Raiatea]..., by William Hodges, 1774. Exhibited at the Royal Academy in 1777 this is William Hodges' largest painting recalling sights from Cook's second Pacific voyage, in this case a 1774 review of a Tahitian war fleet. Ministry of Defence Art Collection. BHC2374

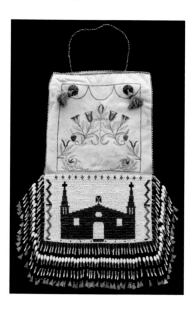

ABOVE AND RIGHT: **Métis shot pouch**, from Manitoba, northern Canada, collected by Captain (later Admiral Sir) George Back, between 1819 and 1834.
AAA2644

Deir Kadége.
noon — 1.P.M.
Jany. 2. 1867

(28)

Find Out More

Collections Online: collections.rmg.co.uk

Although over 1.5 million people visit the Museum each year, millions more do so on online. The Museum's Collections Online pages comprise an ever-developing catalogue of the collections at various levels, from basic records of an item's existence to detailed description and discussion of them. Searches can be made individually, or by thematic or subject groups. The website's Researchers pages also give access to related resources, including the Museum library and manuscript catalogues, and other electronic aids (although some subscription web resources can only be used, free, from the Caird Library itself).

The Library and Archive: rmg.co.uk/researchers/

Over two million documentary items are held on the main Museum site in new, modern Caird Library and archive, opened in 2011. These include books, manuscripts, ephemera, prints and drawings, charts, maps and atlases. They can be found using the online cataloguing systems already mentioned and, in most cases, pre-ordered online for inspection, in advance of a visit. (Ship plans and photographs are not held on-site but arrangements to see them can also be made.) The reading room is open to all, with resources for many sorts of enquiry, including family history. Users only need to show formal identification to be issued with a Reader's Ticket.

Learning at the National Maritime Museum

A year-round programme of activities for all ages explores the collections, the site and the themes of the Museum. This diverse programme includes film seasons, conferences and lectures, study days, workshops, performances, and tours covering art, science and history. So whether you want to study astronomy or explore Britain's encounters with world cultures there is something here to inspire you.

PREVIOUS:
The Queen's House, built by Inigo Jones, 1616– c.1638. The only surviving building of the former Palace of Greenwich, this is the main showcase for the Museum's art collection. The Royal Observatory can be seen on the hill in Greenwich Park behind.

OPPOSITE: **Deir Kadige**, Egypt, watercolour by Edward Lear, 1867. PAD9103

First published 2011. Amended second printing, 2012,
published on behalf of Royal Museums Greenwich by
NMM Enterprises Ltd.
All text and images
© National Maritime Museum, Greenwich, UK, 2011
with the exception of pages 40–41 © Science & Society
Picture Library, National Railway Museum collection

National Maritime Museum
Royal Museums Greenwich
London SE10 9NF
www.rmg.co.uk

ISBN: 978 1 906367 52 7

With thanks to the Royal Museums Greenwich authors:
Robert Blyth, Quintin Colville, Jenny Gaschke,
John Graves, Gillian Hutchinson, John McAleer,
Pieter van der Merwe, Nigel Rigby and Claire Warrior

Project managed by Lara Maiklem and Diana Christou
Edited by Pieter van der Merwe
Designed by Nigel Soper
Photography by Tina Warner and David Westwood
Production management by Geoff Barlow

Printed in the UK by Belmont Press

10 9 8 7 6 5 4 3 2 1

FRONT COVER: **Planispheric world map**, by Francesco Rosselli,
Florence, *c.* 1508: hand-coloured engraving. G201:1/53A